CLASS ENCOUNTERS

By Maketa Smith-Groves

FREEDOM VOICES
P.O. Box 423115
San Francisco, CA 94142
www.freedomvoices.org
orders@freedomvoices.org

For gamins and gamines, everywhere.

Table of Contents

PEOPLE
Anarchists and Lovers

PLACE
Los Angeles

PEOPLE IN PLACE
Teens Inside the System

PLACE IN PEOPLE
Detroit

PEACE IN PLACE

People
Anarchists and Lovers

City Girl (1969)

I was born for the City.
I don't have country eyes
—though they're nice.

They look too
fast
to seek
where danger lies.

19 years of City
 makes me: unnaturally fast
speed and cars are all I know
 the best things in my past.

But
I'd like to trip through meadows to know
what meadows are
I'd like to trade
the city
one night
for a country star.

But
I'd go back to cities,
and
I'd go back to bars where drunks in wine
and ruin
flicker out, like country stars.

Heart and Soul

For the old ones who peer at us
through ancient eyes
wondering
pondering
if they are seen at all

their eyes that see more from memory
than sight
wondering
pondering.

Their movements/slow/shambling
impede others who refuse
to lend a hand or offer a step
in rhyme with theirs

for the old ones. . .
to say
they all have love and food
to say
that pigeons are not their only companions
and that myths
about cat food are only myths.

For the old ones. . .
who pass the afternoons
on city park benches
for the old ones
who shuffle along city streets clutching
small items in paper bags
who wear heavy coats in summer
and walk with canes
the jaundiced-eyed ones
the shaking hands ones
the ones who practice yoga
swim laps

the ones who believe they will be saved
and
those who believe nothing at all.

For those who live alone.
die alone proud or humbled
laughing at death/or crying

I would love to write a poem for every line
every wrinkle every history
every varicose vein
and
liver spot.

For those who dance. slowly
alone in the dark to the music
of their youth
Internal/Eternal
music.

For the Heart and Soul of America
for those
who have worked all their lives
enriched this nation that doles out nickels
and dimes
for the fruits of their labors
purchase of their souls
and
leaves them alone and stumbling
in rented rooms with no heat
and
little prospects - workers (no more),

I would love to write a poem
about the heart and soul of America.

Round

There is
a 'roundness' in this world a
'go a-roundness' a
'ball of confusion' roundness
that
it's all happened before and
will happen again roundness.

The round maze
roundness to
confuse our beginnings
and endings
which are always the same
and known by few
so
we are always looking for ourselves
in
the places we left behind.

There
is a roundness
in the all-seeing eye in
the glistening iridescent
bubble released
in the wind.

And if
I'm talking in circles it's because
there
is a roundness in this world that
demands examination that
demands affirmation that
does not adhere to
linear existence.

There
is a roundness in the way this poem may one day
come around
and tap you
on the shoulder when
you least expect it.

For Amiri Baraka

Amiri
when your strolls along sidewalks became nightmare
    affairs
your features mired in shadows
made deeper by others' imaginings,
clenching of purses/briefcases

you patiently crossed the street your only weapon your
    pen
which sought through mind
to transcend the 'now' and
become a universe of righteousness: no easy path
you poet,
you dusky frolic,

and the others so relieved
by sight
of the pale orb
now walking towards, 'the countenance
of familiarity' representing 'safety & security' dazzling:
the brightness of his features,

a known entity that strips
in one stroke of pen
billions of dollars and
transfers it on to
the already filthy and rich
leaving the beguiled smiling wishfully into
the lingering dazzle of his empty sun already
moving past in
preordained orbit.

Amiri,
I understand: you were no more and
no less
than a messenger flying

within your orbit of transmittal

an orbit defined by
flares of conviction
bonfires of hope,
and
five alarms of reality

your orbit created sun energy
your countenance the deep
blackness of space
of
all matter that surrounds
and supports
everything else in existence.

Color (post 9/11)

What is the color of patriotism?

Is it
red, white and blue like
waving flags multiplying, a procession growing
larger every day?

Is it the color of
green lawns behind which hide good people
afraid to be really good?

Is it the color of
green money
used to purchase
justice?

All around
colors grow deeper and silence becomes
huge, spaces in between
sound bites lengthen
as does loneliness.

What is the color of patriotism?

Is it truly black
red brown yellow white,
or is it a combination of the above?

Is it gray like the clouds that hang
over the silence
or like the troops
with their tanks rolling in formation

the buzzing of their steel gears
a symphony of terror to
the inner ear?

What is the
color of Redemption?

What is the
color of Silence
cutting
sharp as a knife?

Angry Black Women

(Post-Civil War records reveal the prevalent belief among white women of the period, that raped black women enduring slavery, were "responsible for the rape.")

In this beast the US
of America where
we've toiled out our life's blood

toiled impossibly to make possible
what others simply could not

black women earnest in
determination, have carried our
'born disadvantaged' children
and
the children of others
to a nearly impossible awakening
of maturity and survival.

Denigrated by all for asking
men to give us what others
receive most naturally (respect),

we've had no time to play coy
demure
or otherwise manipulate
the emotions of men

we've had hungry babes to feed
and
ways to pay rent to figure out

we have never been considered
"trophy wives" yet
our minds/ bodies
have been used by all alike

are we angry black women?

From the dregs
we have become poets
politicians/opera singers/scientists/
astronauts/doctors
majors in a system
that would
gladly ignore us.

We carried a civilization
nearly lost
on our backs and knees
to a "new world"

yet

the most acknowledged:
our lack of ability
processing 400 years of neglect
in
a single lifetime
for
the arrogant types to be comfortable in a
'passive presence' of black female 'type.'

Are we angry black women?

Niggah

Black American mouths spout the aberration, "Niggah"
as wild mushrooms sprout in
spring fields.

Young and old
mouths that would hunger for words of justice instead
ingest a
steady diet of
racism
and regurgitate it
for generations - sustained with offal for
offal it is,
that raw, hateful word now justified
with black claims of
claiming it for our own
thus assuring its 'neutrality,'

Neutral
only in the mouths of blacks,
therefore,
not neutral at all.

Stop Mass Incarceration

In the hours
between waking and sleeping
there is
only animal instinct
to eat
to drink
to void
to be cautious, wary
of shivs and rape

tattoos work outs
contraband (disallowed)
smokes (allowed)
& sad weary visitors

 even the
 strong men cry, whisper "oh mama"...
 droplets of spittle
 from
clenched jaws
stifling anguished prayer.

U.S.A.

(For Amadou Diallo, Sean Bell, Aaron Campbell,
Oscar Grant, Trayvon Martin, Andy Lopez, Eric Garner, Tyrone
Brown, Michael Brown, and sadly many others.
(1991, revised in 2014)

I know
you will say, we are all one
under our skins,

that I can expel my breath
and
have nothing to fear.

I know
you will say, we are all one under our skins but
Your Eyes Burn Crosses as they seek
to tell me all is well
Your Eyes Burn Crosses AND
you have NEVER stopped lynching
black boys and men
in Mississippi California Alabama Florida Missouri New
    York Ohio. . .
and wherever.

I know
you will
tell me
all is well. . . but. . .
your eyes. . . burn.

Anarchist's Credo

Names
are the beginnings of obligations:
go without
refuse introductions remain 'strangers' no strings.

Be careful of strings be sure you want them casual
introductions are
without merit
formalities required by society -

to go
without a name suggests fluidity,
vacuity of motive

more humane
without introduction
beings have no need for
masks of 'politeness'
you can always greet
without exchanging names

Do it.   Feel it.
walk away without a name - don't break
the spell of 'being'
look back without a name:

you know who you are, anyway.

Anarchist's Credo 2

I am granite stone
an obelisk of granite stone
monument
to the unconvinced

I am concrete
a building wall
a mountain terrain
boulder at the bottom of waterfall
city sidewalk cradling broken head

I too, can be a killer

but my weapons are words
listen closely
move nearer
hear the irregular ticking of
my killer heart:
my weapons are words
adoration for the natural world

I am rosewood unyielding granite stone
my weapons are words
adoration for the natural world.

Boy at War

You didn't want to be released from
the land of living
because
you were too young anyway
to go off into
that other place.

You found your way back through memorial stone

and let us know that
you were once elemental
and romped as a child and
made love
as a teenager in tall grass and
drank beers with your boys and
didn't know sometimes and
were always
a little bit brave and
often scared.

So you went to other tall grass and
laid down, and
never got up.

We need to remember that

because you were so young and fresh
and
liked your girl so much and
loved your mama
      and
the smell
of fresh cut grass in the summertime.

The Poor

The poor are broken down all over the world: Hobbling
    Danish grandmothers pushing grand-babies in
    busted carriages filled with foodstuffs

Austrian child's life plan plotted by age 10 skill
    level/development rate 'determined'
system sends some to university, most to trade labors.

Roma gypsies living under bridges in Stockholm:
    washing clothes in canal waters, while people 'with
    money', expressions controlled, wander food aisles,
    seeking that, they can afford.

In Copenhagen the poor are scouring the trash for cans
    and bottles, as they do in all cities of wealth, in all the
    world.

We are all over the world, we poor.

Deeply etched lines invade the faces of young mothers,
    and deepen with each dollar, kroner, peso, pound,
    and euro
paid to the handlers of wealth.

Asian drunks and homeless are seeding on
the steps of the train station in "Wonderful Copenhagen"

The poor are broken down all over the world: broken
bent withered
but not spent -
and growing more aware
with each indignity we suffer.

Legacy

The Wasted Earth will bear no more our
human efforts

She will bear no more our vanities
our hapless failings

a twisting cruelty: our blighted time on Earth
our
venal indifference to
all that sustains us,

our Mother Earth will sing no praises
will begin anew
her own protection
her own survival

and we
we humans play no part
in her plan.

Old Shoes

There is always that person
a bit outside the circle
of knowing.

When others lean
to the right she leans
to the left: her orbit elliptical words burning
in atmosphere.

No matter how fervent the passion
other fuel is needed
to keep a love going.

Outside the circle she burns cold
never knowing the touch
offered so freely to others
perhaps less worthy.

She is worthy but unskilled,
her love crude as old shoes.

Memory
(For Flemming)

Having met such a fine and
centered man

I am a much more fine and centered woman.

Each day traces
like a shadow
to original form these lessons you left

these
fine and centered perceptions
each movement a memory
clear and sharp like bird beaks bird wings
fine things like
the legs of a crane as it moves
with slow grace among
the thrashing reeds.

Basic People

We are
basic people. . .

and as such are
bark and peat moss   rock
and boulder swamp
and sky.

My friends when I meet you
on the streets of this
and
all cities,

when we speak of bread
and care and loss and love
and politics and art
and toothaches triumphs births
deaths, please see me
know that I see you and
even with
our complexities

we are all basic people and
I love you

for that.

Math Lesson

The bar graph of
my emotions indicates
today will be a good day.

The line across your forehead
indicates otherwise.

So it goes on this way
towards infinity
two intersecting theorems
of infinite chaos.

Security

The conventions of your life
kept you honest - a good father
sometimes a good husband
but
always honest.

So honest you revealed the affair
compromised safety
disabled chances
for
slipping to old age
with remnants
of emotional "security"
leaving you now
to understand: honesty endures,
while security is shadow
that moves through
our lives
on occasion
turning to light.

Best of Friends

We are
the best of friends even when
we're apart there is
this connection: we are
the best of friends.

We are moving towards
something slow and easy
as
a southern river
drowsy and peaceful as
honeyed tea.

To Live Among Demons. . .

sprinkle them with love.

Not love of them or their deeds

but

the love you carry as
a magnet
in the soul

for those yearning
for the riches hidden deep within
the valleys of heart.

Something About The Sea

There is something about the way
the waves roll in undulating...

Something about the way
the spume slithers back from the shore...

Something about the way
the rocks are patient with the frenzied surf...

Something about the way
birds play tag with the sea... (for promise of fish)...

Something about the way
seaweed lies exposed in the sun...

Something about the way
fog hovers just above horizon...

afraid to touch down, afraid to let go...

that is something close to how I love you.

Untitled

For love incomplete unanswered
there is no path/silent corridors

yet words flow
undammed waters
rushing
clearing paths in its wake.

As love destroys, so it creates:

when foolish hearts
beat their last,
pages burn with life.

Lover

During play your face
a hard mask
   melts as wax
into soft lines of acceptance of
what we create together:
a line of truce/ no warlike
after behavior:

your surrender is
my silent joy.

Wild Card

You are a wild card a terrified mule afraid
to go forward not wanting to go back,

frightened   bucking
quaking
denial
and need to be happy... and...
you   are   most dangerous
when happy.

Angst Divas

Angst Divas
bow down
to the blues lose ourselves in
"oh baby, I done you so wrong!"

Find salvation in Billie Holiday
Patsy Cline
Edith Piaf
Bessie Smith
and
sad men with
sad lessons all over town.

A flash of tight skirt his
bared chest with
just the right hairiness
turns everything upside down again
"oh baby, just let me get close to you" works every
time, and we are convinced
like a long playing
stuck on stupid.

Angst Divas bow down
to the blues lose ourselves
in "sweeter this time"
I know it's got to be.

Angst Divas find ourselves
staring down into midnight
when
what we sought was the sun.

Madagascar

Birthplace of my ex who spends his days
driving taxi in
the fast lanes and heat
of Los Angeles.

Madagascar, I imagine you are lush
a reflection of the beauty that is Africa
as my ex was and is.

Song to Carmelo

You sing to me of love every day
I hear you
in small spaces veiled
by silence of the wind
rising
of the wind's suspirations
pauses and wanings.

You sing to me of love every day
in the wings of the butterfly
in slow motion of swallows
swift movement of hummingbird
arc of the hawk sunlight
on wing.

You bring me joy in the shadows
of the mountains
water fall free flow
and
the munching of tiny creatures
in tall grasses.

You bring me joy.

Place
Los Angeles

L.A. Poem

"Show Biz kids making movies of themselves,
you know they don't give a FUCK about anybody else."
-Ricky Lee Jones

At Noah's Bagels/Ventura Boulevard
having breakfast   trying to read
attempting
to understand the day,
girls plopped down at the table
closest to me: every word a scream in the
confined space

the "show biz kids," 19 or 20 years
discussed Saturday night vomiting bouts
at a J-Lo party
and how disgusting and
rude they were and
their subsequent hangovers-

all with giggles, of course.

They excoriated one another
and
everyone they knew and
complimented each other on their nails and
reminded each other
to call "Jose" whom they'd met at J-Lo's.

They said "fuck"
36 times and giggled 500.

The day started at 90 degrees and
progressed from there

So,
when the woman bumped my table with
her cart full of tin cans her gray hair so visible
her face so worn and

her apology so sincere,
I accepted   watched
as she averted her eyes
and mumbled the same to
the "show biz kids" whose mouths
fell
at my eye contact with 'her,'
    too much class encounter
in close-up.

When she left all I could think about
was her exposed head
and
ask myself
why
have I stayed here so long?

Not here, at this table but
in L. A. county, and
I told myself it's because for every
'Lindsay Lohan wannabe'
there is someone like that woman
who also needs recognition
whose eyes become steady
whose troubles
dissipate momentarily in
return of a smile.

Then
staying is vindicated- the crowded freeways
encroaching fires
hell-fire hot summers the rehab babies
movie star wannabes
terrified elderly drivers
endless reports

of blood alcohol levels
DUI accident stats and

gangs on gangs
are nullified.

Besides
I'm trying. . .
and therefore determined
to grow lotus in whatever patch
I'm given.

Braceros

You came
to
work the fields
to break the horses
to smell wild flowers and dream
of
beautiful brown girls you left
running down
Mexican mountainsides their laughter
as motes in
piano wind.

Braceros
you came
to rope the calf
neuter the bull and
dance
in one bar towns where
sawdust is thrown to floor nightly
to catch the beer sloshed from mugs
as you weep into one sleeve thinking
of your girl but pretending
you are laughing your way into
el Corazon
de Los Estados Unidos.

On 8th and Alvarado Streets

Where Latino and Korean cultures
collude and coalesce:
stringent sidewalk sharing
and
downtown skyline ill formed
   missing shape of mortar,
stands stark
in a pungent sky,

I saw on one bike
four kids
riding hell
out of two wheels
silhouetted at hill-top
against broken skyline.

Gave me laughter
and delight
to write something magical,
real about the
City of Angels
to write:
I was heartened:
such balance
such cooperation
such balletic poise,
glad the four
were not engaged in the
behaviors'
popularized by media
the
  ghetto stereotypes so often
found
in the images of poor L.A. Youth

no reduction to lowest and common
denominations here
just kids
trying and doing (yes, unsafe)

but

trying and doing
and
doing well.

Street Scene

It is dusk/my favorite time/except here
the cars zoom across wide valley streets
more like a big ole town/than true urban sprawl
bleak/deserted of walkers:
those who civilize a landscape.

Kerouac called L.A./ "the most brutal city
in America"
possibly noting the red sky makes it seem
we have all died/gone to a hell presided over
by sleek
beautiful cars that rule the landscape and
are
barely held in check/by acid lonely men
and women done up in glitter.

Smashed Pumpkin

Walking down an L.A. street early morn
raggedy man ahead of me
in conversation with self.

Raggedy Man in the middle
of the sidewalk as I pass
say,
"good morning" acknowledge
his willingness to be there
when so few are.

Raggedy Man in Santa hat
gap toothed grin wide
all over his face
wide as smashed pumpkin.

Hello, Santa Claus!
his reply
both of us standing
in Santa hats lone walkers
on L.A. Streets laugh aloud
laugh and laugh each recognizing
fringe element
when we see it.

Walkin' on Raggedly Man shouts,
"Merry Christmas To You,"
'And to You, Sir,'
I say walkin' on with a wide grin
all over my face
wide as smashed pumpkin.

People in Place
Teens Inside the System

All Life

Sometimes
without knowing the details
we sense
the violation the pain sometimes
we become aware of the guilt
if ever allowed
there was pleasure for just one second.

All life is this way:
everyone
everywhere wishes
there were things that hadn't been but are
and
we are ambivalent sometimes
about our feelings towards those things
those times
and
I see it now in your eyes:
remembrance and fear
that remembrance makes it right
when all remembrance does
is make it less.

Anything for Love

Children do anything for love:
children kiss the brutal hand for love
children run to please for love
children shut doors for love
children won't tell for love
children repeat the same in love
Children do anything for love.

Don't Take to The Streets

Don't take to the streets
they will wear you out
leave you
staggering in their alleys
leave you
staggering in their capacity
to totally diminish.
Don't take to the streets
they will
leave
your body brutalized by necessity
of need
leave
your mind demoralized
by
what you will see and do
they will scoop out your soul
and
inhabit the shell.

Don't take to the streets
no matter what they promise
no matter the fine thugs standing around
with hands out-stretched offering brain candy
and
fast easy money: it won't be fast,
it won't be easy.

Don't take to the streets
Don't take to the streets
because. . .
The Streets Never Take to You.

Ed

You are big and shambling
and
on your lucid days
you speak freely
of rough
and
live wire sex.

But on
the bad days
when the sickness takes you
and
the meds numb you down to nothing,
I sit and
speak quietly to you:
human/harrowed/hull
waiting patiently to be filled again
with lewdness and
wild despair.

Leaky Nets

My hands are jugglers,
juggling water
and fish
for the hungry

my eyes are two bleeding holes
swallowed by misery want neglect

my heart a mass at times, weak
other times, a great engine

my legs
are locomotives cranking
transporting fish
I catch

children are the fish
children are the hungry
my hands
are
two leaking nets.

Children of the Barrios/Ghettos

Children of the barrios/ghettos
you are hunted like animals
cut down in youth   guns put in your hands
by adults who
like Romans in the arena await
your fall
replay your mistakes
on automatic repeat.

Though all
I have are two eyes
two arms
two legs,
I won't let you fall.

I can't let you fall I so badly
need to see you survive
if only to show that not all adults
are maimers and monsters.

Children of the barrios/ghettos
little innocents
hardened stone cold
I see each of you
as a star: beautiful, adrift in space.

Li'l Tony

Li'l Tony at age 16
is one hell of a trooper
with his tiny head: when I saw it propped against
his pillow,
I thought it was
a doll's head

and his cerulean eyes round and glassy with
no bottom lids and
teeth that whistle sometimes
when he talks.

All the Boys

All the Boys play
Beethoven's Fifth.

Each one sits spritely
seriously quickly tinkering
the moody cloud.

Each one with
his own reasons for choosing that piece
each one pulled low into
the deep notes.

Each one approaching the piano
the way a tired person approaches a bed
the way a thirsty person approaches water:

All the boys play
Beethoven's Fifth.

Jewel

Lil Jewel
child
of the Eastern sky,
bright eyes glittery
as
crowded stars straining
against
each other for attention
brilliant and bold
her eyes:
dancing orbs scorched with
vigor pirouetting from body
prancing on desert sky.

Bad Attitude

You inspire me with
your raw energy and
your raw rage and
your raw clinging to life.

You inspire me with
your
bad attitude and
your shoddy ways bad habits
that make you willing to live.

I appreciate anything
that gives you ability
to survive anything that feeds your
will to battle.

You inspire me.

Essence

Davone. . .
Your
mental stability is fragile crystal.

Your kindness an albatross
your emotions, a storm at sea.

Yet. . .
if I were lost and
doomed to fail
I would want   you
near me because
you are
an essence of innocence and
one who
breathes
forgiveness.

Holiday Blues

Holiday Blues. . . have you careening down
the hallways screeching punching
at your incarceration as though
it exists
in human form:

in a matter of speaking,
it does.

It exists in social workers probation officers
youth counselors and parents
who left just after your birth or
took a flight out
some years ago, leaving you to these hallways,

and

the blues you screech
in
major keys.

Scarification

She has attempted to erase
the scarification of her life
and
replace it with
scarification of her arms.

Bloody youth file through,
bodies bearing
wet/red proof
of
poor adult protection.

The macabre rite of passage
done in secrecy
and pain,
bleeding
through their lives
will not bring
the pride of scars
worn like crowns in Africa.

King of the Hoop

King: he's on top of
the basketball hoop pole.

Yesterday, the doctor was uncool
telling him of his bad heart
results of the EKG,
the inebriated lines.

It's bad enough to give up
the game of football and
live in a group home.

And
to end up on top
of the basketball hoop
with staff screaming:
"come down, you'll break your legs"
when you know they mean their hearts,
gives you satisfaction/at least
for the moment/bad heart and all.

Ragged Little Puppet

(In memory of Antwone, who was killed in a car
wreck during an unauthorized leave from facility)

On the roof you traipsed pouting
wanting to hurt us all
declaring yourself ready to jump.

Possibly
you would have broken
an arm or leg maybe both.
But you would have survived,
and
in any case
the roof is not where you were supposed to be.

We enticed you with everything we could find but
only
the ragged little puppet from
my handbag
with the googly eyes drew you closer
drew you down to walk away
needing to complete puppet's hairdo
and
to scold.

Place in People
Detroit

(Detroit – French origin:
means a 'strait', or limited in space or time)

Detroit

You ascend/descend with
barbed wire and
2'x4's plunged into your
crushed skull buildings.

The death you sought was beautiful -

(the death you found, unforgivable.)

Ode to the Beatles

Because
my guitar gently weeps I wept
19/and so in love or/so I thought and
George Harrison's guitar sang for me
when things were tough

many long and winding roads took me
to some places I wouldn't
go today
knew no fear then
knowing the path paved with mercy

the octopus's garden
is where I tried to be
at the end of each day young
facing a careless world

I wanted to wrap the world in peace
I wanted to give the gift of hope to
every broken soul I met

I wanted a world without
borders or nations
I wanted mercy and truth
a world without hunger
homelessness or greed –
Just imagine.

Diaspora

My mind has a landscape that could not form
anywhere except America.

This is the Diaspora
the vastness in my soul
like an African desert
forever roamed:

This Detroit memory of
my father's
twelve gauge blasting
away wall/and blood splattered rats
my father's rage that he could not prevent
this horror/this poverty/cleaving
as
Mississippi mud and
KKK raids
cleaving.

Shooting rats late at night
rats the size of footballs
scampering over sleeping bodies of
siblings and I
this profound rage and
desecration by the rats
(for sleeping children are sacred ground)
filled me with my father's rage
and
I have raged ever since.

Life. . .

is a fragile thing
clandestine life running through
as ice cream runs through our fingers
dripping
running
we lick
we lap
lest we miss its flavors.

Life, being a durable thing:
the tastes linger
stains remain.

However Described

I was born at the time
when ticker tape ruled Detroit
when cars rolled off the line in
syncopation exact
to each moment of the day.

Cars that made the world
led the Industrial Revolution,
technology that enabled war
strengthened metallurgy
and sped fossil fuel consumption
infrastructure building
enriched our lives
rolled us from coast to coast.

We
who were growing up in the midst
loved and hated it.

Detroit/Manchester/Pittsburgh/Liverpool
Gary
and all industrial towns in
all the world
I have forgotten or never knew,
carry this stamp
sometimes called authentic (harsh)
Heartland
rooted (harsh)
down-to-earth.

There is no way to fully explain
 how
 it was growing up
 in that environment:
 triumphant

to survive/perhaps

animal-alert/visceral/haunted/
street-wise
future PTSD
are
some ways described by survivors because
we know
we never again want it,
nor wish it upon others.

Whatever it was.
However described.

Them Two

(This poem is written in the Appalachian vernacular so often
heard during my childhood in Detroit)

Jim and George (George was a girl) come to die
in Detroit appearing one day mysterious
and
slow moving symbiotic with molasses
from Georgia   Appalachia
or from
wherever the hell they came
come to Detroit in 1969
Detroit
whose streets were flooded with methamphetamine
(but no problem)
every factory town got to have it for 60 hour
work weeks

and
them two never dressed like
ordinary hippies: no bead light
no glow light
no feather/leather/rainbow
or
earth light.

Like country bums they wore
faded grays and blues slouching hats
dilapidated shoes
colorless featureless waif
beings
dropped as from a cold
and windowless distance
inhabitants of asteroids
and
other dead things in space
or

only half survived from

coal mine country/soul-sucked/seeking death.

Hearts bursting into bloom of death
as roses burst into life,
we were called, the activists/pacifists
black/white/in between commune dwellers
to bring order to a scene
of bursting hearts/literally
in a locked room
in a house of red.

We yelled,
"call the Police!"
after pummeling fist falls
on locked door
and
snuffling animal noises inside
no need
or ability
to allow entrance.

Them two
hearts bursting, this is their song
the only one they'd want sung:

Jim and George: never really knew them/
and
don't know why
but
in 1969
they come to Detroit to die.

For Smokey Robinson

Oh-h, baby, baby. . . reading your life story
was taking a step back in time/to when nappy
headed pubescent girls swooned in Detroit
second story bedrooms at mention of your
name waving freshly painted fingernails and toes
in the
Detroit summer air
keening to the sound of your voice:
warm and lush and
sliding over us
as Aunt Jemima syrup on
Sunday morning pancakes.

Oh-h, baby, baby . . . like every girl
on the block
I had a monster crush on you, and Lord
you sang like you had seen it all
with
much pressure to bear
to stay alive and make it
a young black man in Detroit
lookin' so fine and
walkin' so fine and
writin' from your heart.

If love and pain could be bottled and
sold for elixirs,
Oh-h, baby, baby,
we would have all been cured.

Hastings Street

(This poem is written in the street patois I, and
most black children spoke, during my childhood
in the inner city of Detroit, Michigan.)

Hastings Street got
rib joints/fish shacks/it got
live chickens/barbershops (with lye, for a 'process')

Do you know Hastings Street?

Hastings Street got
beauty shops/juke joints and
John Lee Hooker and
B.B. King and
sidewalks crowded
with
pimps and hos and
children of pimps and hos who better not
even think of going into their parent's professions
having schooling as an option.

Do you know Hastings Street?

Hastings Street got
'sissies' who sit on stoops
with the women
and gossip
(they were always accepted in my
neighborhood) and no 'straight man'
would make an insult
knowing
Hastings Street Sissies' strait razor
is
always sharp, always handy.

Yes,

Hastings Street got violence unspeakable but

it also got love innocent gentle fine
like baby fat.

Hastings Street got demolished.

It
got demolished flat down
to nothing.

Did you know Hastings Street??

Em

(For Eminem)

rage is white consciousness
rising from
black cauldrons of Detroit

view is smoking end of gun
used often in
bar fights over forty-five dollars
and
a pretty woman.

reality is
gleamed through
factory smokestacks
cold streets
tears
lost love
warm beer spilled
money spent
women whored
workers indentured
and
blues sung.

Life without
music
is cold:
cold
as Detroit city
with
rising winds off
Canadian Shores.

Appalachia Story

Timothy had a thyroid the size of a baseball
poking out on the left side of his neck.

Timothy was 19, and from Kentucky

John wore a colostomy bag and
without thinking, I was insensitive and
kept talking about how "gross" certain things are.

John was 23 and from
West Virginia

Timothy and John grew up on
bacon fat on bread and
little else, and
Ethel,
from Tennessee
who managed to reach age 92 in Detroit, apologizes
all the time for being
from the 'hollow,' though
(she pronounced it as the "holler"),
apologizing
as though
coming from the holler means
she is the one
owing apology.

Motor City 5

All sinew/hair/bone/ The MC5
take the stage in clothing more lacquer than cloth

they prowl, eyes behind dark glasses framed
by
long/black/tresses
peer through the crowd as x-ray through bone

cacophony of sound unmistakably theirs:
no other urban cry so primal on these shores.

The hall is rocking/The MC5
sway their bones inside their jeans/they pounce
on their guitars/they prowl
the stage:
unearthly loud
and
utterly irresistible.

All She Needed

The defiant girl met us
under the marquee of the
Grande Ballroom announcing
MC5 TONIGHT!

Her Eastern European parents,
Czech or Polish, did not know she hiked her
long skirt
up around her waist revealing
her thighs and
pulled out
the knot of bun at her neck allowing
her hair to waterfall.

We climbed on stage, her parents' fear
of 'contamination' to their daughter from
Western values of little concern as
she led the way to dance in front of
giant speakers saying
all she wanted was a little more freedom,
all she needed was a little
more freedom.

"Godfather of Punk"

Iggy Pop in 1968
Saugatuck, Michigan,
you first performed your little trick of
leaping off stage.

Godfather of Punk,
we punked you in those days:
saying 'hell no'
to your leaping act, we parted like waves
and
you dived
in our midst only to hit floor bloodied and
repeated this act every time
as
did we
all unaware
you were simply leaping
to get upstream (as you eventually did)
and we,
we small ripples,
we were not meant to carry you.

Fever

Most beloved art created in Detroit
comes from
a coiled place in the soul
a hungered place of truth
seeking beauty dance of creation
with
signifying hands and
elegant feet
a coition
a wrenching
a moan
the hunger
of a lifetime an
ever grasping hand an
ever receding light
a fever
that continues
beyond measure.

Monster

Hulking bulk Detroit City, built from
blood and spittle
bolts and pistons
southern lynch mobs
and
survivors of the lynched/lynchers
sweat of Eastern Europeans
and
Appalachian poor, rose up
writhing in poverty heaving in anguish and
did what was asked for decades.

For decades /producing /one third
of
gross national wealth
hulking monster now lies
in ruin.

My monster of childhood
dreams/nightmares
lies in ruin,
now
it is stripped of everything:
larders plundered waters polluted

now we realize the worst
Free Enterprise
can offer.

Owners/plunderers have taken their booty and fled
yet
they can't run fast enough
or
far enough to evade this Monster:

It is embodied in all of us: Chevrolet
Mustang   Cadillac,

General Motors, Ford,
even
Deuce and one quarter:
concepts from Detroit
ingested with
mother's milk.

Muse

Detroit City
it was not safe to go
even to your college bars
after a certain hour.

Yet
I loved you
loved your disquiet streets
your unwavering despair
in the face of ruthless automation
and
your belief it would
go on forever

Yet
it was killing your people
in too many ways to count-
and you Detroit,
hurt me to the last hour of my life there.

I often
loved the drama yet
mostly dreaded what could come
what you were
 and now. . . what you are.

Detroit City I fought you I fought your cruelty
while loving you
and because
I fought for body and soul
down to the core:

I can't stop fighting
not now or ever

Detroit, your gift to me:
a legacy of
strength
joy
fright
music
wounds
and
poetry.

Peace in Place

Tree on the Side of the Road

You are cool and ancient as time
bountiful cloak
black shadow of tree.

Long ago
you began to give back your life
leaf by leaf
and
now
lean with
coal black dirt at your roots
deep imprints
of those who stopped
to inhale your beauty.

You have the only cool place
in town, and
I lean into
the fullness of your grace,
caress your bark
color of human hair.

Sea

tonight
the full moon clasps
her pearl halo 'round the sea

the massive surf hugs
the shoulders of shore

the silt foam a
bubbling brilliance
beneath our feet
a sweet susurration

and
extending to horizon
shore to shore
comes the milky mist.

Winter . . .

is the time
when
great sorrows come to visit
and ravish
like birds of prey.

This is the dampening down time
the season of winter
when weariness of
what years have wrought
hangs in the air/haunting
dense
as winter fog.

With a Child's Excitement

Flying high above water creates jagged patterns dragons
rough edged triangles translucent pools.

Look!
   How roadways line the earth!

Wiggly Squiggly pathways
through the land.

Look!
   How clouds lay above the earth:
suspended in air/fat like frogs!

Look!
   How I fly above the land great eruptions
of mountains below
snow crested sublime!

Waters

Lake Bodensee juncture
of Germany/Switzerland and
Austria
hosts the River Rhine
tumbling waters
as the Rhine slips
to lake bed flowing silently/obscured
mystic/unique/commanding/primeval
temporary dependence,

and love affair of waters
with an entering into
and exit of.

In The Garden. . .

dappled sunlight forms
eco-bridge between worlds of dawn
and darkness

coastal morning glory lift budding heads
lovers of the sun   rise
at arrival of beloved orb
all soft petaled/dewy

it is this time/place
of all things, perfect
for an instant,

green foliage
soft petals
hues
liquid sunlight.

Arboretum Experience
(Ann Arbor, Michigan, 1970)

In the light of the full moon
we transformed/our day shapes
falling away
to night shapes/nymphs
fairies
(a few gargoyles
and trolls, perhaps) tip-toeing
frolicking
joining hands 'round
rose bush/crocus vine,
pagan delight!

Dancing nude
on summer night in silent circles
homage to peace
and
the night and/also to this
garden delight:
we were unseen
flesh making merry.

Silver disk moon evaporated
at dawn,
and only then we dressed
silently,
slipped into
sleek cars owned by the day.

En Barcelona I

The sea air:
a sweet caress
across my skin/it hugs
and whispers.

En Barcelona II

The day opens the birds' beaks peacefully
the sky with stealth brings rain
a curtain of water on façade of buildings
wet worn steps of market place.

En Barcelona III

Every day
I go to the sea
to the gild of
the water,
glinting knives of wave,
spume crested layers
children at play
languid swimmers
with
a gentle rising and falling
of arms.

Cry of Gulls

Come down to the sea while
she still floats
her beauty in lacy
covered waves
her peaks frosty blue
capped in white.

Come down to the sea
while we have beach
Enough to share fine glassed and
beige-sanded with gulls above.

Come down to the sea
while she still lives/already
she has shed her tide pools
her little creatures: sand crabs
and jellyfish gone,
her beaches bereft
and bare of bounty.

Come down to the sea
while there is time/uncertain future
has not claimed her yet
and
all my vistas turn to her
while she still lives,
and always
always,

I remember
the cry of gulls.

Drought

Strangled stalks rustle dryly
burnt husks
stirred to life by
tines of the wind
an emergence of sun
a rainfall of zero
a thirst of the land.

Night

warm blackness wraps round us
soft as
a velvet cloak.

Night envelops shadows
as fog envelops hills.

About the Author

International poet Maketa Smith-Groves, a native of Detroit, Michigan, has lived in California for many decades. For her first collection of poetry, *Red Hot on a Silver Note* (Curbstone Press), she received the PEN Oakland/Josephine Miles Award. In 2014, she was honored with the Acker Award for exemplary Avant-Garde excellence. She currently divides her time between the U.S. and Europe.

www.ingramcontent.com/pod-product-compliance
Lightning Source LLC
Chambersburg PA
CBHW032222120126
38151CB00009B/133